AT HOME W
English 2

Louis Fidge

OXFORD UNIVERSITY PRESS

Notes to parents

How to use this book:

- This activity book has been designed for children aged 6-7, to help support their work in the second year of school.
- It is intended to be fun to work through, so that the child goes off to school feeling that they enjoy reading and writing.
- Though most of the tasks can be done unaided by the child, you may want to help with reading the instructions, discussing how to do the task, and filling in the results.
- The book is deliberately self-contained, requiring a minimum of further books or paper.
- But it should be treated as a springboard to further activities off the page, using all the language opportunities that exist in the world around the child.

How to help your child:

- Don't expect your child to do too much at once; they can pick single pages that appeal to them, and work in short, keen bursts of activity.
- Help your child by discussing the activities, how to answer them, and what to write down.
- If your child has difficulty with an activity, don't make them anxious about it; check whether they have a recurrent problem with a particular skill, or let them just move onto another activity.
- Give plenty of praise and encouragement.

What is the National Curriculum?

- The National Curriculum offers a framework of content and skills in different subjects for children aged 5-16.
- This series is designed for the 2 years of Key Stage 1, ages 5-7.
- Each subject is divided into Attainment Targets, which define the knowledge, skills and understanding in that subject; the grid on page 64 shows how the activities in this book relate to the Attainment Targets in English.
- Children progress through different Levels of achievement, and these books cover the Levels appropriate to Key Stage 1.

What will my child get out of this book?

- Children should enjoy filling in each page of this book, and making it their own record of achievement.
- There is a 'traffic light' in the bottom corner of each page for self-assessment: your child can fill in 1 if they enjoyed the activity a little, and up to 3 points if they enjoyed the activity a lot. This will indicate to you their particular strengths, likes and dislikes.

Contents

Capital letters	4-13
Alphabetical order	14-19
Books and reading	20-25
Fun with food	26-33
Handwriting	34-41
Word play	42-51
Writing	52-57
Hare and Tortoise	58-63
National Curriculum grid	64

Capital letters

Trace over each letter, then write one yourself.

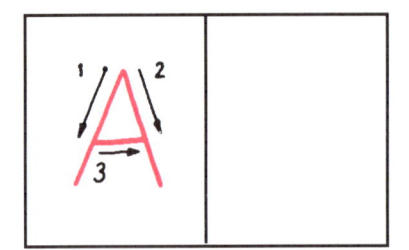

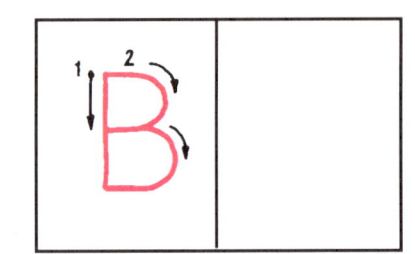

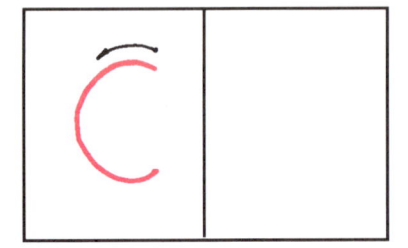

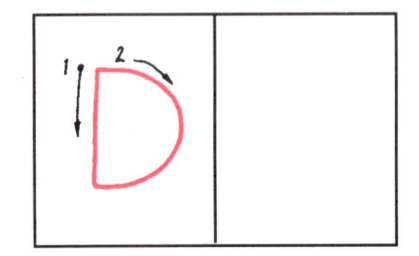

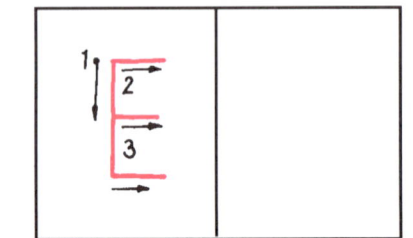

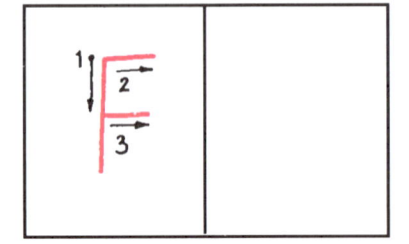

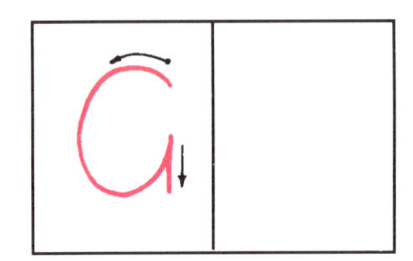

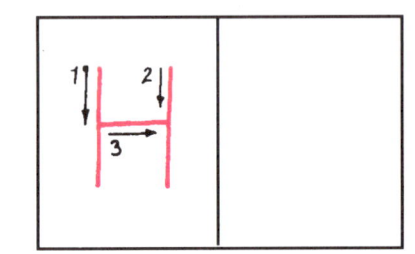

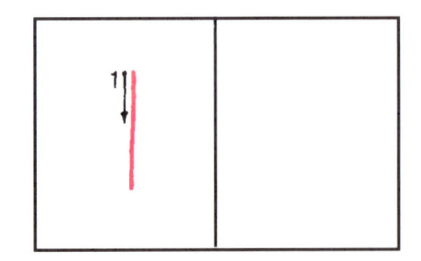

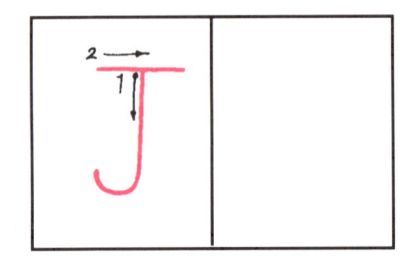

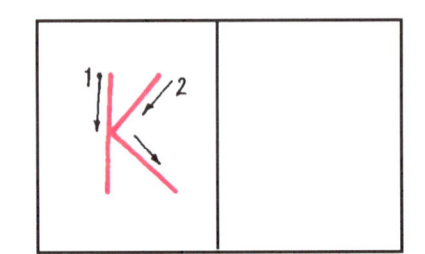

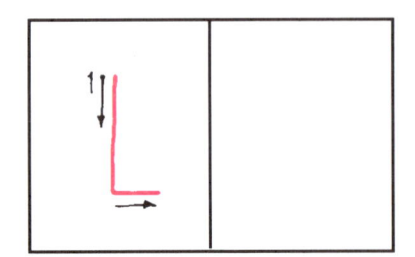

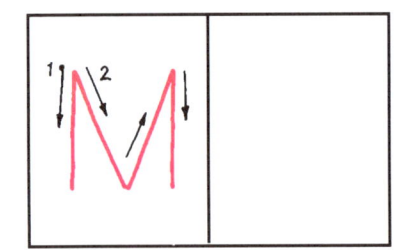

N O P
Q R S
T U V
W X Y
Z

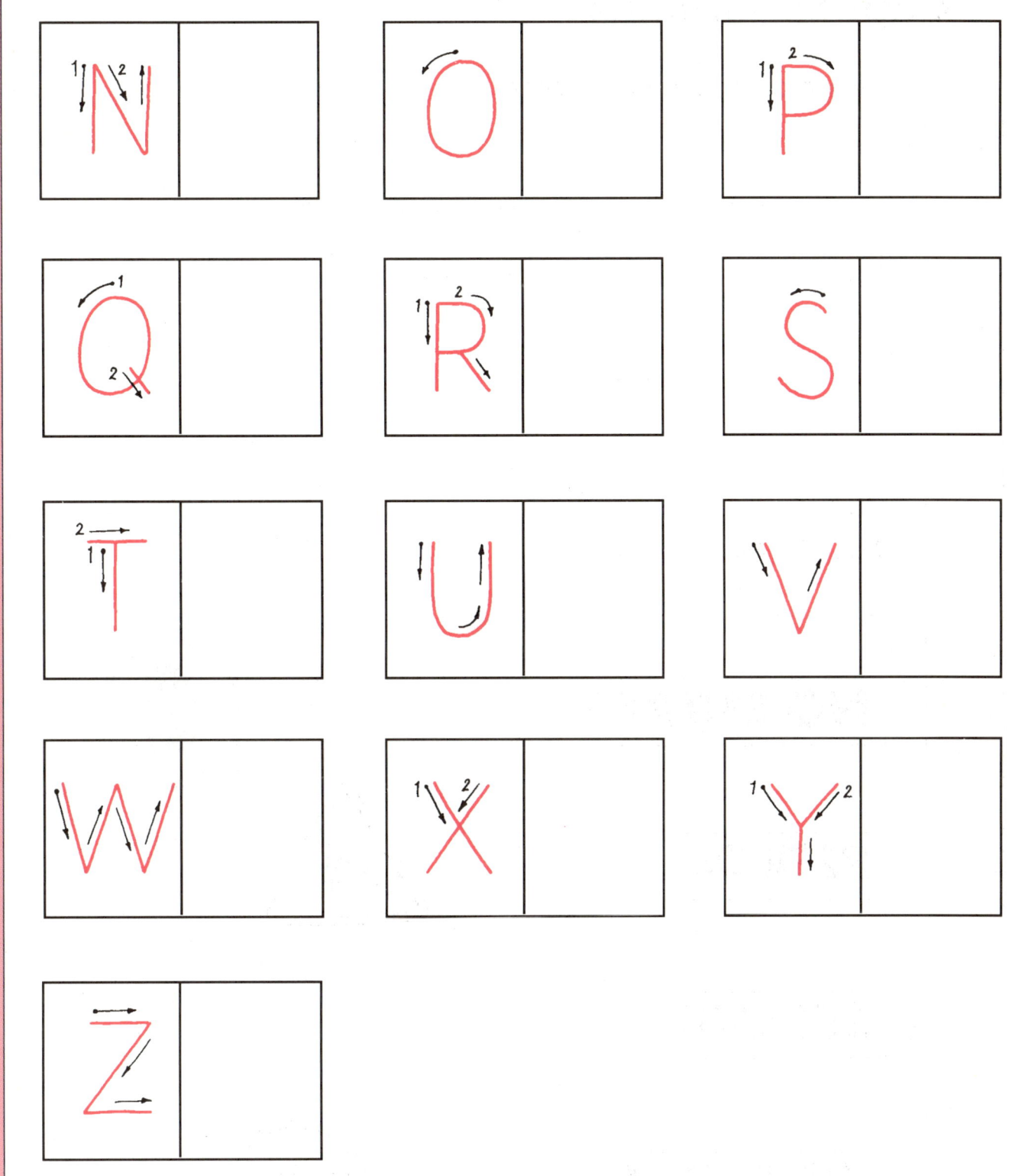

Capitals on signs

What do these signs say?

TICKETS

EXIT

SUPERMARKET

WC

DANGER

Match these signs.

NO ENTRY

PETROL

SCHOOL

ONE WAY

Write signs for these shops.
Choose from the words below.

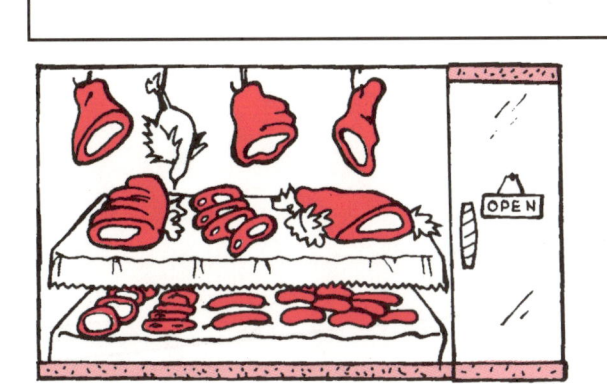

FISH
BICYCLES
GROCER
SUPERMARKET
BAKERY

VEGETABLES
BUTCHER
TOYSHOP
CHEMIST
HARDWARE

Capitals in headlines

Newspapers use capital letters for headlines.
Draw a picture for each news story.

DAILY NEWS
LION ESCAPES FROM ZOO

DAILY NEWS
SCHOOL BURNS DOWN

DAILY NEWS
GRANDPA WINS RACE

DAILY NEWS
HURRICANE HAVOC

8

Capitals and small letters

Put the cars in the right garages.
Match the capital letters to the small letters.

Capitals for people and places

We use capital letters for people's names.

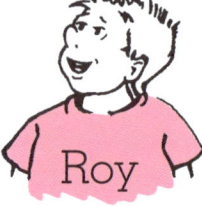

Anne   Roy   Sushi

Write some more people's names.

_____   _____

_____   _____

_____   _____

_____   _____

We use capital letters for places.

London   New York   River Nile

Write some more places.

_____   _____

_____   _____

_____   _____

_____   _____

Can you write a name and a place for each letter of the alphabet?

	Name	Place
A		
B		
C		
D		
E		
F		
G		
H		
I		
J		
K		
L		
M		
N		
O		
P		
Q		
R		
S		
T		
U		
V		
W		
X		
Y		
Z		

Days, months and sentences

The days of the week start with capitals.

Monday Tuesday Wednesday
Thursday Friday Saturday Sunday

The months of the year start with capitals.

January	February	March	April
May	June	July	August
September	October	November	December

And sentences start with capital letters.

This sentence starts with a capital.
It ends with a full stop.

Start with capital letters

My name is ....

I live in ....

Today is ....

This month is ....

.... month will be ....

We go on holiday to ....

My best friend is ....

My school is at ....

My birthday is in ....

My favourite day is ....

We don't go to school on ....

Remember the full stops!

Alphabetical order

Try to answer the questions without looking at the alphabet.

1. Which is the first letter of the alphabet?
2. Which is the tenth letter of the alphabet?
3. Which letter comes next to last?
4. Which letter comes after 'O'?
5. Which letter comes between 'U' and 'W'?
6. Which letter comes before 'S'?
7. Which letter means a line of people?
8. Which letter comes between 'J' and 'L'?
9. Which letter means me?
10. Which letter is round?
11. Which letter means a kiss?
12. Which letter becomes 'V' and 'X'
13. The second letter of the alphabet is...

| Aa | Bb | Cc | Dd | Ee | Ff |
| Gg | Hh | Ii | Jj | Kk | Ll | Mm |

14 And after that comes... ☐

15 What noise does a snake make? ☐

16 Which letter comes after that? ☐

17 Which letter is number 13? ☐

18 And the one after that... ☐

19 The fifth letter... ☐

20 Between 'F' and 'H'... ☐

21 The fourth letter is... ☐

22 Two letters after 'S'... ☐

23 Three letters after 'K'... ☐

24 Letter number 6... ☐

25 The one before 'I'... ☐

26 Which is the last letter of all? ☐

Now look at the alphabet to check your answers.

Colour in a square for each right answer.

N n	O o	P p	Q q	R r
S s	T t	U u	V v	W w
X x	Y y	Z z		

Bookshelf

These books are in alphabetical order.

A. Ahlberg   E. Blyton   R. Dahl

Don't forget to use the authors' surnames.

Can you write names on the other two books?

Write in some authors' names from your own books, in alphabetical order.

These books have fallen in a heap.
Draw them on the shelf in the right order.

J. Murphy
M. Rosen
L. Fidge
S. Hughes
H. Oxenbury
D. Bellamy

Which authors come in the first half of the alphabet?

Which authors' names have just one letter between them?

Where would you put a book by Richard Hughes?

School register

Here are some names from the school register.
Look at the order of the second letters!

J. Adams						
B. Appleyard						
J. Bond						
D. Costa						
P. Crisp						

Write down some names from your class, in alphabetical order.

Dictionary quiz

These words are listed in the dictionary in alphabetical order.

sandwich

sausage

seal

shark

ship

shirt

shoes

snail

socks

spider

strawberry

sweets

Which words are things you eat?

Which things would you find at sea?

What do you wear?

Which other words are animals?

Books I've read

What are your favourite books?
Draw their covers, and write why you like them.

Now, for each book, draw or write an advert to make someone else want to read the book.

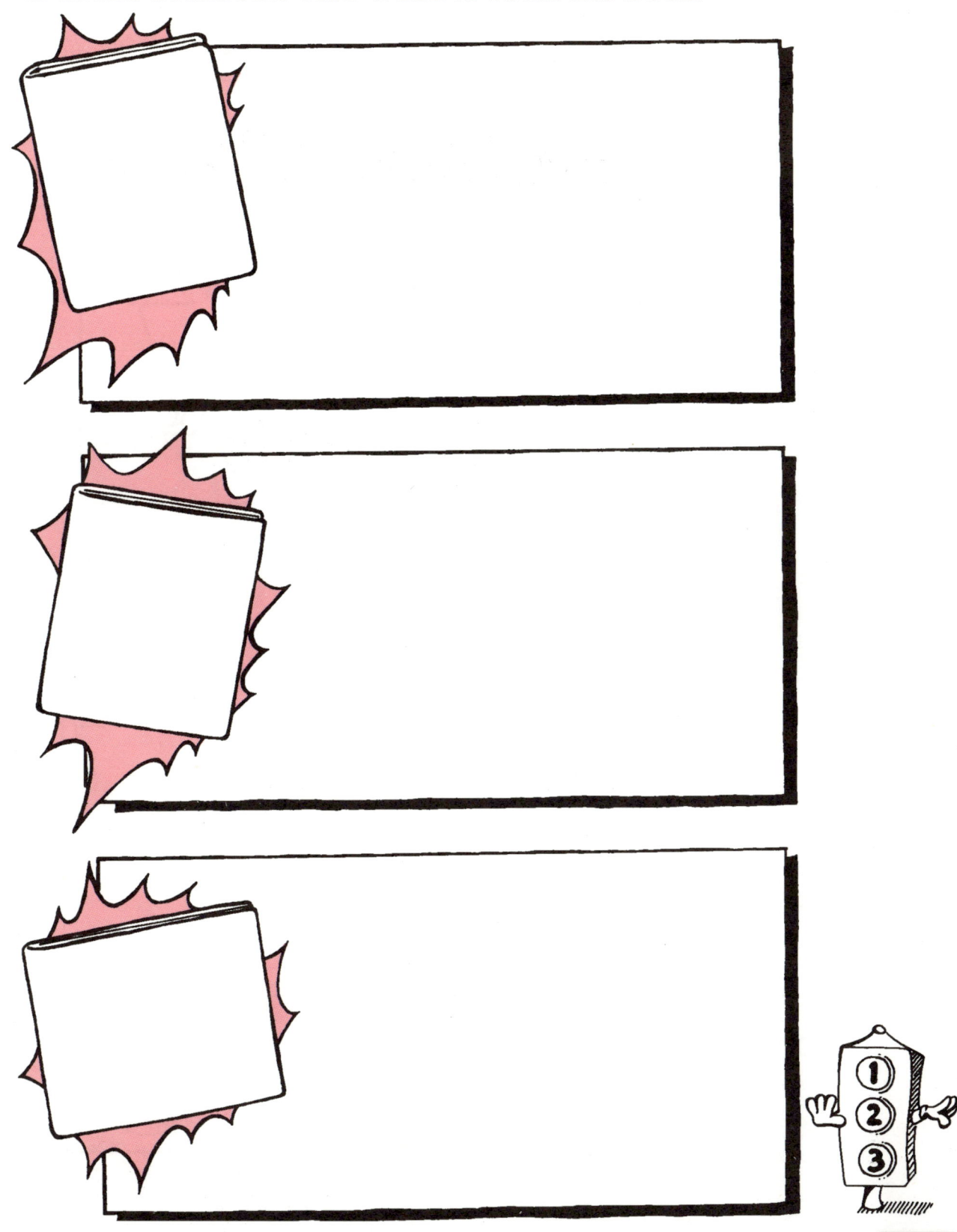

Parts of a book

These are some of the parts of a book.

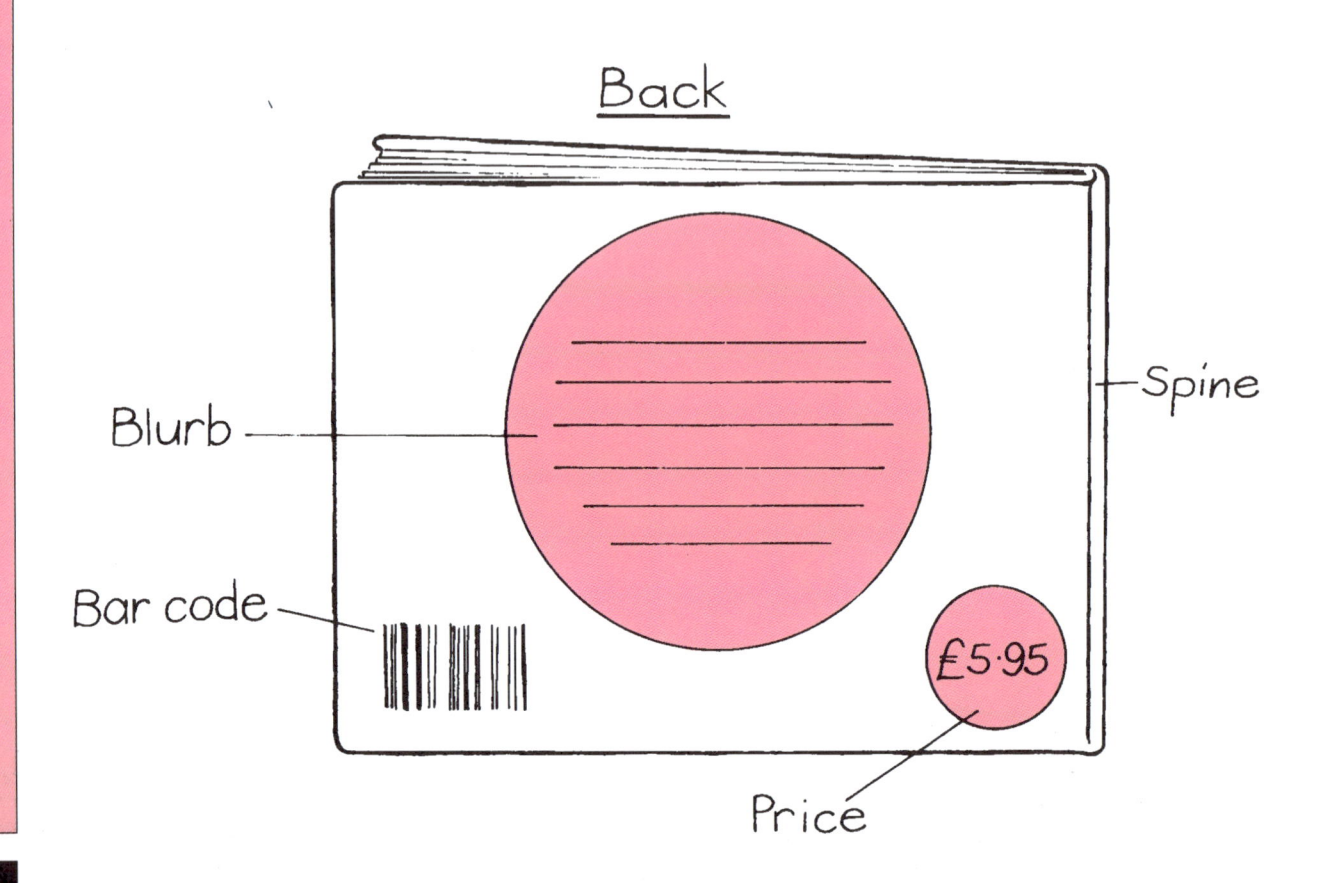

Front

- Publisher — WALKER BOOKS
- Title — Five Minutes' Peace
- Author — Jill Murphy

Back

- Blurb
- Bar code
- Spine
- Price — £5·95

Fill in the names of some of your favourite books.

Title

Author

Publisher

Title

Author

Publisher

Title

Author

Publisher

Finding out information

How do you find out information from a book?

You read the title.

You read the contents page.

You read the index.

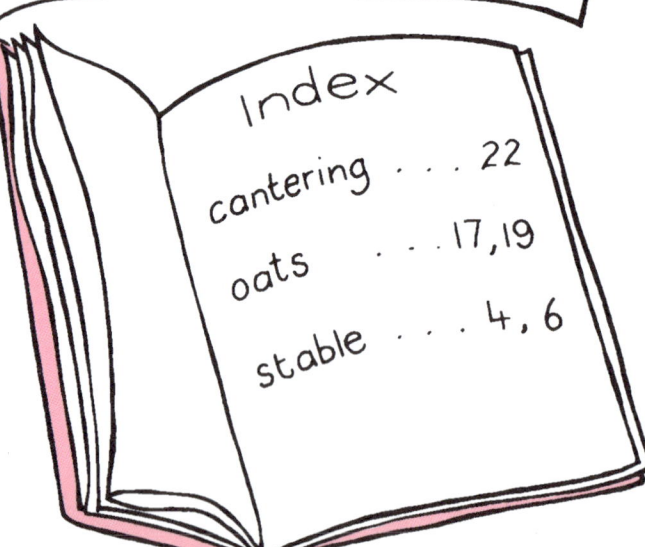

Find an information book at home.

What is the title?

How many chapters does it have?

What page is the index on?

Where does chocolate come from?

Here is some information about where chocolate comes from.

Cocoa beans grow on a tree.

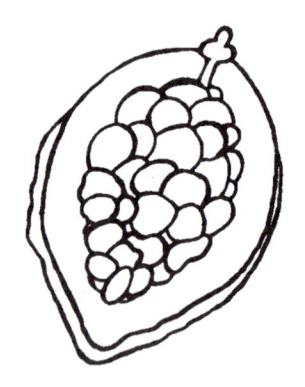

The pods are picked and cut open.

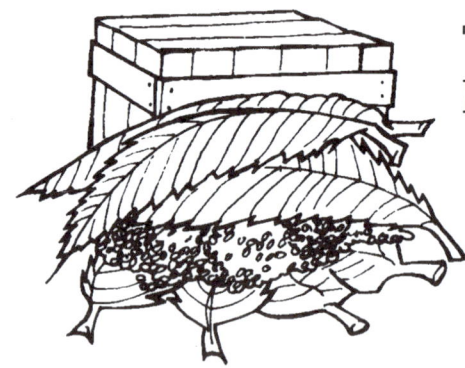

The beans are left under leaves, or in boxes, to grow ripe.

Then the beans dry in the sun.

The beans are packed in bags, and sent off by ship.

Then the beans are roasted.

The shells come off.

The beans are crushed.

The cocoa is now ground into liquid.

It is heated, cooled, and rolled into bars.

This is how you get plain chocolate or milk chocolate.

Reading a recipe

Banana pops (for 6 people)

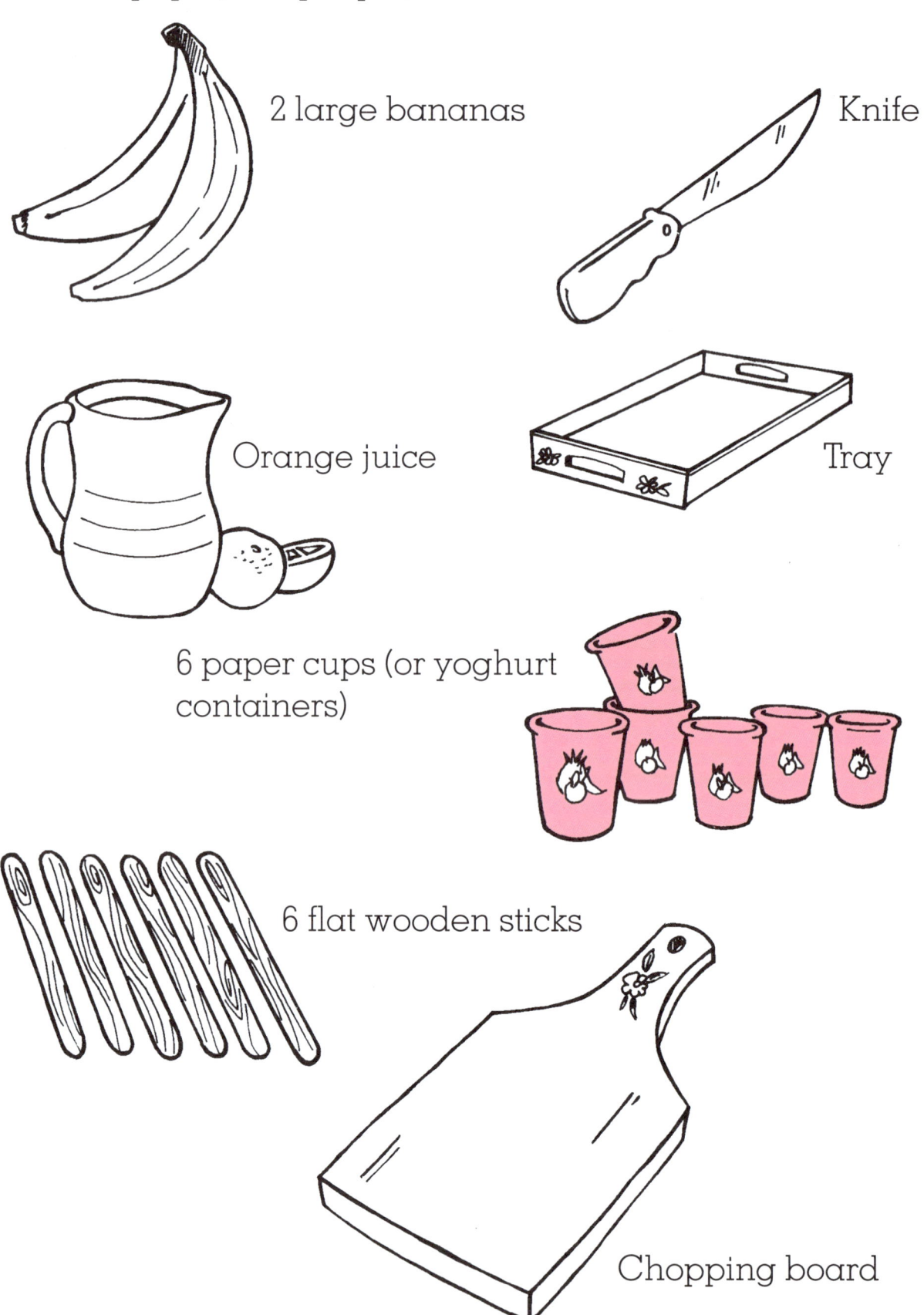

2 large bananas

Knife

Orange juice

Tray

6 paper cups (or yoghurt containers)

6 flat wooden sticks

Chopping board

Wash your hands.

1. Peel the bananas.

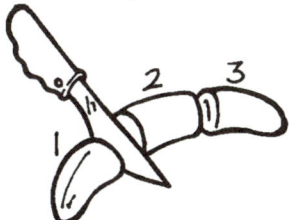

2. Cut each banana into 3 pieces.

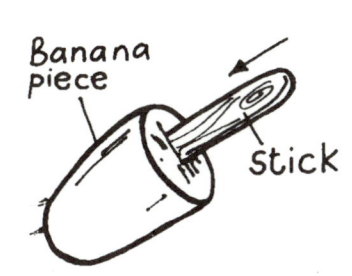

3. Gently push a stick into each piece of banana.

Banana piece
stick

4. Place each piece of banana into a cup.

5. Pour in orange juice so that it covers the banana.

6. Divide the juice among the 6 cups.

7. Put the six cups into the freezer until set.

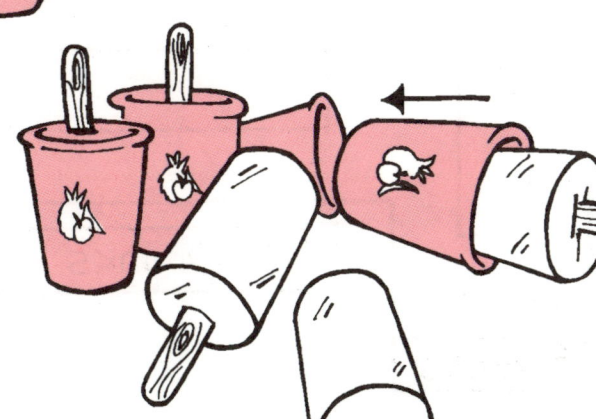

8. When set, remove the paper cups.

29

Supermarket shelves

You need to buy these things in the supermarket.

- oranges
- ice-cream
- bacon
- chocolate cake
- orange juice
- toffees
- carrots

Draw your route to the right shelves.

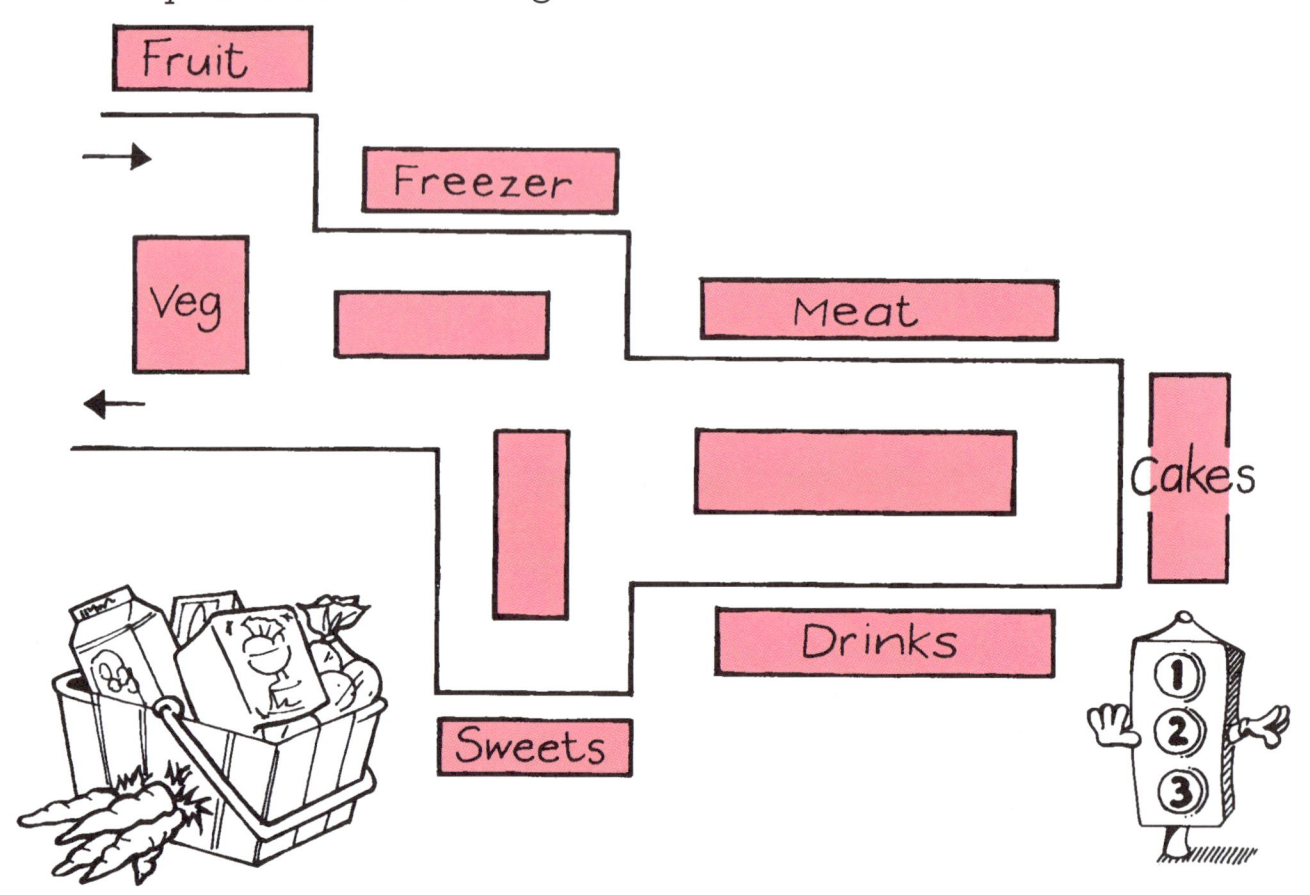

Fruit

Freezer

Veg

Meat

Cakes

Drinks

Sweets

Shopping lists

Make a list of
3 sweet things you could buy:

3 things you could buy for breakfast:

3 things for a baby:

3 things for your pet:

Food alphabet

How many foods can you think of beginning with each letter of the alphabet?

Here are some pictures to get you started.

A a B b C c

D d E e F f

G g H h I i

J j K k L l

Mm   Nn   Oo

Pp   Qq   Rr

Ss   Tt   Uu

Vv   Ww   Xx

      Yy   Zz

33

Handwriting

in *in*

tin *tin*

bin *bin*

a tin in a bin

a tin in a bin

it *it*

lit *lit*

hit *hit*

sit *sit*

I hit it

I bit it

uu uuuu uu uuuu uu uuuu

ut ut

hut hut

nut nut

pull   bull

35

aaaaa aaaaa aaaaa

am *am*

dam *dam*

ham *ham*

Baaaa!

lamb *lamb*

stamp *lamp*

all *all*

tall
tall

small
small

a small car

a big car

a

a

a big star

a small star

a

a

37

sad sad

draw

glad glad

draw

and and
band band
hand hand
sand sand

a band in the sand

et *et*

net *net*

pet *pet*

Write some more 'et' words here.

This unusual animal has *This*
one head, nine eyes
and ten legs. Draw it here

Whooooo an owl hoots

an open door

some toys on the floor

red red

run run

row row

ring ring

wet wet

wild wild

wheel wheel

wing wing

Words that are ill!

Add these letters to the pills to make some new words:

b f h k m p t w

....ill ill ill ill ill
....ill ill ill ill

Write the words you have made in the bottle.

...ill Words

Can you make up a sentence with some of the words in it?

Where do they live?

Send the rockets to make some new words!

_____ end   _____ end

_____ end   _____ end

_____ end   _____ end

_____ end

Write all the 'end' words you have made in the rocket.

Throw the snowballs

Throw the snowballs and make some new words.

bl ow
sh
gr
sl
yell
thr
wind
foll

Write the words you have made in the snowman.

Can you make up a sentence with some of these words in it?

44

Jigsaw words

How many different words can you make?

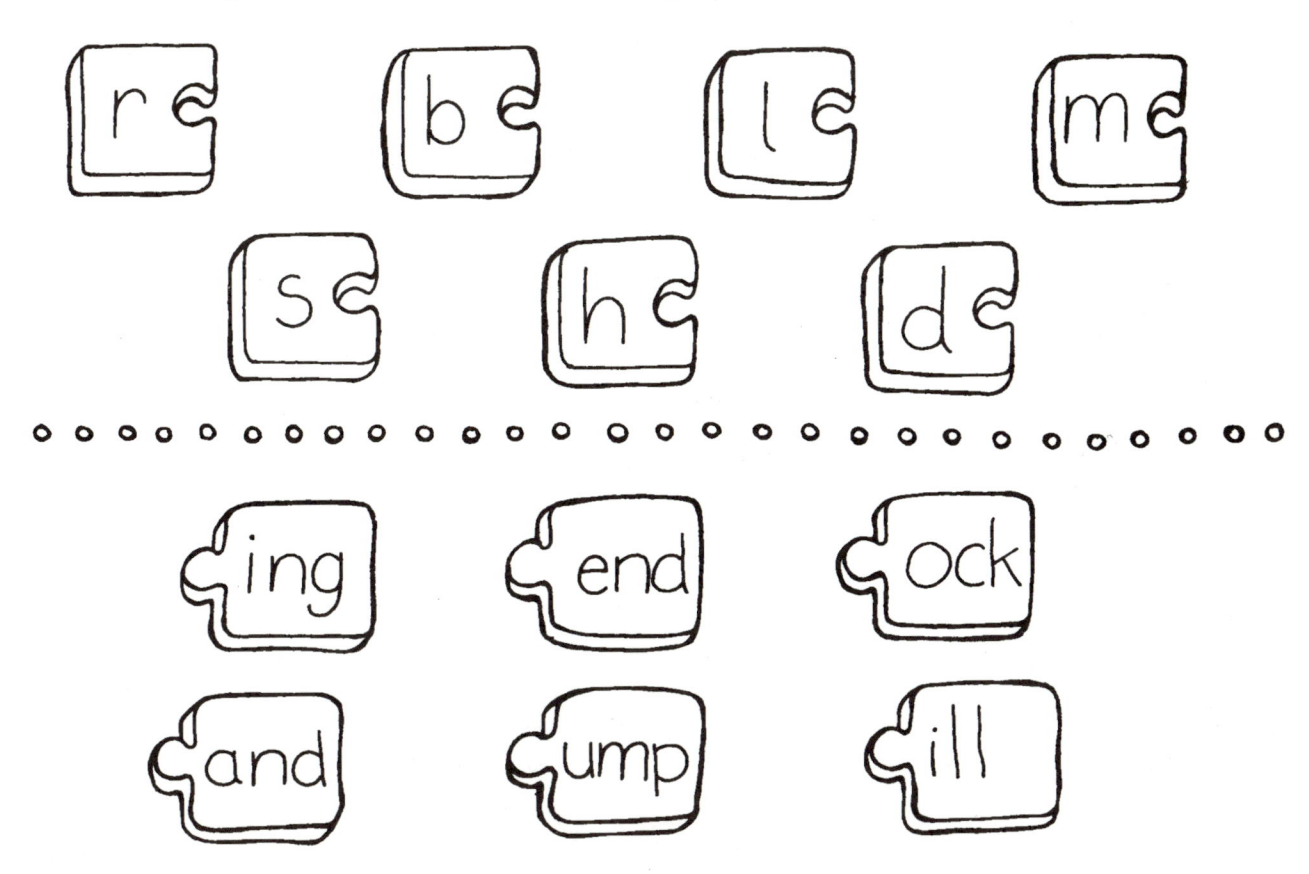

| r | b | l | m |
| s | h | d |

- ing
- end
- ock
- and
- ump
- ill

Write your words here.

ring   hand

How many words did you make?

Long vowels

The magic **e** turns a short sound into a long sound.

hat → e → hate

Write in the new words.

bit → e → _____

mat → e → _____

fat → e → _____

fad → e → _____

hop → e → _____

cut → e → _____

pin → e → _____

not → e → _____

The middle letter which changes its sound is a **vowel**.

The vowels in the alphabet are:

a   e   i   o   u

Plurals

Most words just add **s**, when you have more than one.

cat   cats   pear   pears

boy   _____   girl   _____

stick   _____   kilt   _____

These words add **es**, so that you can say them easily.

box   boxes   fox   _____

cross   _____   bunch   _____

These words are quite different:

man   _____   child   _____

Word magnets

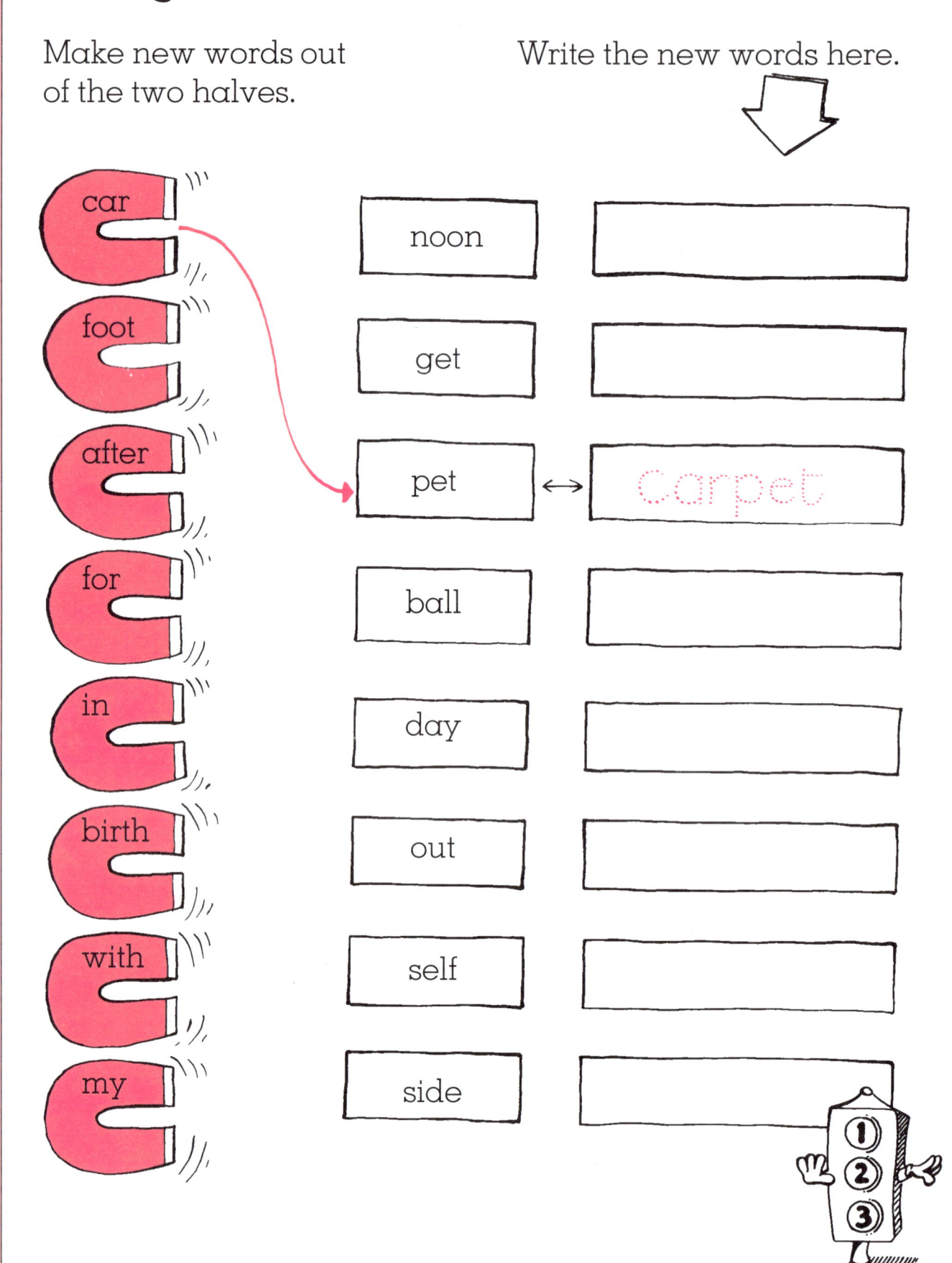

Make new words out of the two halves.

Write the new words here.

car	noon	
foot	get	
after	pet	↔ Carpet
for	ball	
in	day	
birth	out	
with	self	
my	side	

48

Befores and afters

How many words can you think of beginning with:

tele_____   in_____   ad_____

_____   _____   _____

_____   _____   _____

ex _____   pre_____

_____   _____

_____   _____

Look in a dictionary for more words!

How many words can you think of ending with:

_____ful   _____ing   _____ed

_____   _____   _____

_____   _____   _____

_____es   _____ly

_____   _____

_____   _____

There are lots of these!

Hidden words

Inside a long word, you can often find small words hiding!

t e l e v **i s** i **o n**

is **on**

What small words can you find in these?

chair

cup

saucepan

brush

curtains

broom

window

carpet

ornament

Are there any small words hiding in your name?

50

Word shapes

Guess the words hiding in the shapes.
Match each to its outline.

decorations

stocking

snow

friends

holiday

toys

parcel

gift

Writing letters

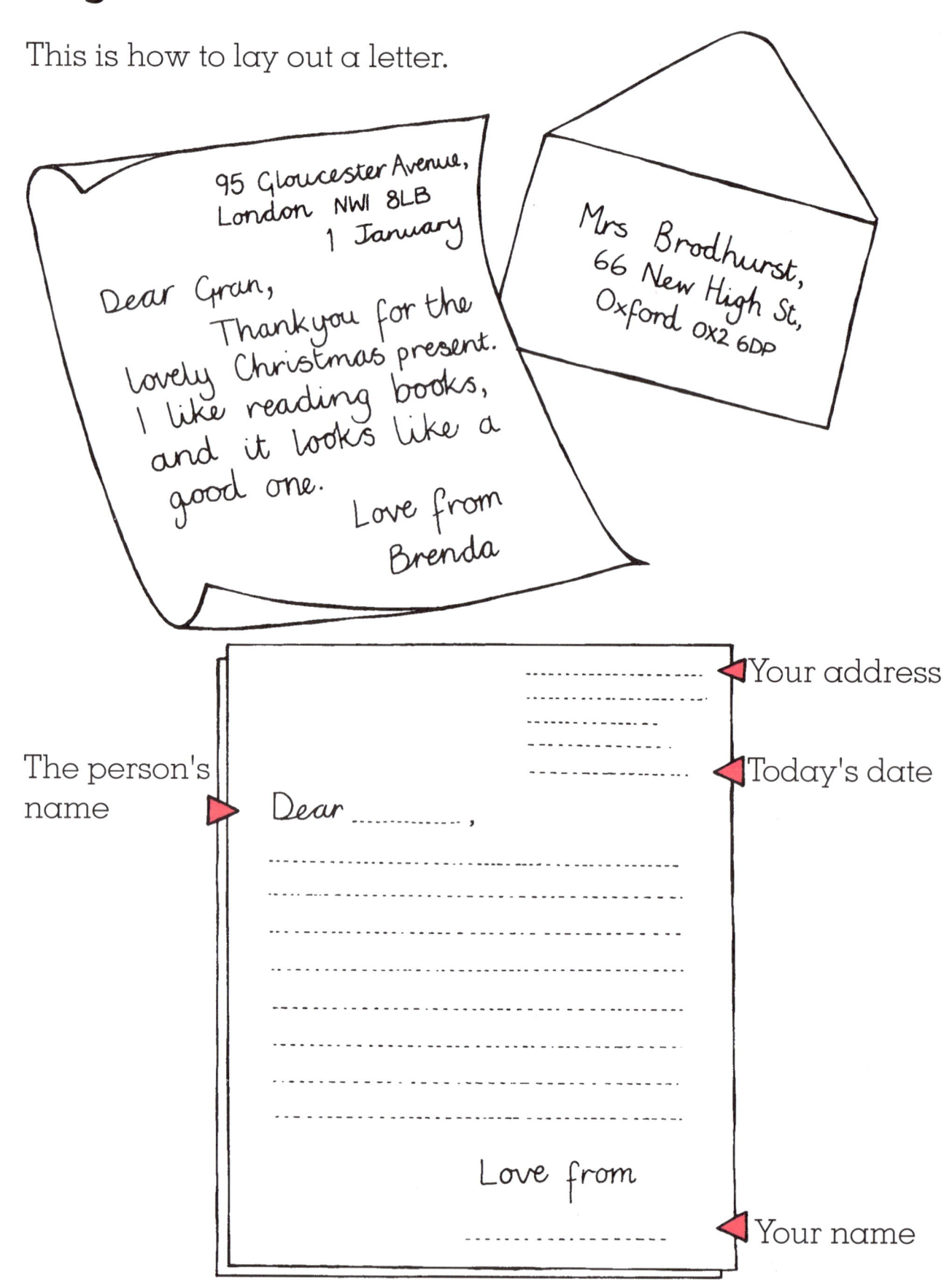

This is how to lay out a letter.

95 Gloucester Avenue,
London NW1 8LB
1 January

Dear Gran,
Thank you for the lovely Christmas present. I like reading books, and it looks like a good one.

Love from
Brenda

Mrs Brodhurst,
66 New High St,
Oxford OX2 6DP

- Your address
- Today's date
- The person's name
- Dear _____ ,
- Love from
- Your name

Write two letters to people you know.
Make one a thank you letter for a present or party.
The other letter could describe
your holidays, or a trip.

Writing a diary

Lots of people write diaries, saying what they've done during the day.

Saturday

Went out to play with Rick.
Bought a new game.
Had beans for tea.

Sunday

Went over to Gran's.
Played in the park.
Dad fell in the lake!

You can write about where you went
who you saw
what you did
or you can describe what places or people looked like.

Monday

It was cold today.
There was ice on the pond.
I wore my red scarf and gloves.

Tuesday

The sun came out today.
We had birds on our bird table.
Our dog ran round and
round the garden!

Write your diary for two different days.
Make one a **real** day that you enjoyed.
Make the other an **imaginary** day, about what you'd most like to do.

Date: _____

Date: _____

Writing speech

There are different ways of writing down what people say. You can write what they say in speech bubbles.

Or you can write it like a play.

Ronnie : Do you come here often?
Archie : Not if I can help it.

Ronnie : Don't you like it here?
Archie : No I don't.

Ronnie : Why not?
Archie : Because the magazines aren't very good...
... and because I don't like going to the dentist!

Tell a story in two different ways.
First, write words for the people to say.

1	2
3	4

Then write it out as a play, filling in their names.

_____ : _____

_____ : _____

_____ : _____

_____ : _____

_____ : _____

_____ : _____

_____ : _____

_____ : _____

_____ : _____

_____ : _____

Hares

Hares are animals which look like rabbits, but they are bigger.

Hares have bigger ears than rabbits.

Hares live alone, not in large families.

They live above the ground, not in burrows.

Hares run very fast, and jump up high.

Tell someone how a hare is different from a rabbit.

Tortoises

Tortoises walk very slowly,
because they live under a heavy shell.

If tortoises want to hide,
they can pull their head and their legs under their shell.

Some tortoises live over 100 years.

Tortoises eat plants, and sleep in the winter.

Tell someone why tortoises walk so slowly.

The Hare and the Tortoise story

1. Hare was a show-off. He thought he could run faster than anyone.

2. All the animals were fed up with him.

3. One sunny day, Hare saw Tortoise. He thought he would have some fun.

4. He challenged Tortoise to a race.

5. Tortoise agreed to race, just for a quiet life.

6. Hare laughed at her and boasted that he would win easily.

7 All the animals gathered to see the start of the race.

8 There was a lot of excitement as they set off.

"Good luck, Tortoise"
"Go on, Tortoise"

9 Hare shot off like a rocket.

10 Tortoise plodded off slowly.

11 Hare ran so fast that he soon left Tortoise behind.

"Look! I'm already miles ahead."

12 Tortoise didn't get upset. She just kept plodding on slowly.

"Slow and sure, that's my motto!"

13 *All this running is making me very hot.*

Hare began to get rather hot.

14 *I've left Tortoise a long way behind.*

When he came to the bottom of the hill, Tortoise was nowhere in sight.

15 *I think I'll have a rest here and cool down.*

Hare decided that there was no need to hurry, so he took a rest.

16

He sat under a tree. Soon he was fast asleep.

17 *Slow and sure. Slow and sure!*

Tortoise kept plodding on.

18 *I'll go quietly here. I don't want to wake Hare!*

After a while, she came to the spot where Hare was asleep.

19 "Slow and sure!"

Tortoise didn't stop. She carried on up the hill.

20

Hare carried on sleeping.

21

It was hard work climbing the hill!

22 "Oh no! Look where Tortoise has got to!"

Suddenly Hare woke up and saw Tortoise at the top of the hill.

23

Tortoise liked going down the hill best!

24 "Well done!!" "Hurray! Well done, Tortoise!"

Hare ran as fast as he could, but it was too late! Tortoise was the winner.

National Curriculum

This grid shows how each activity is related to the National Curriculum in English; it will therefore give some idea of the educational purpose of each activity.

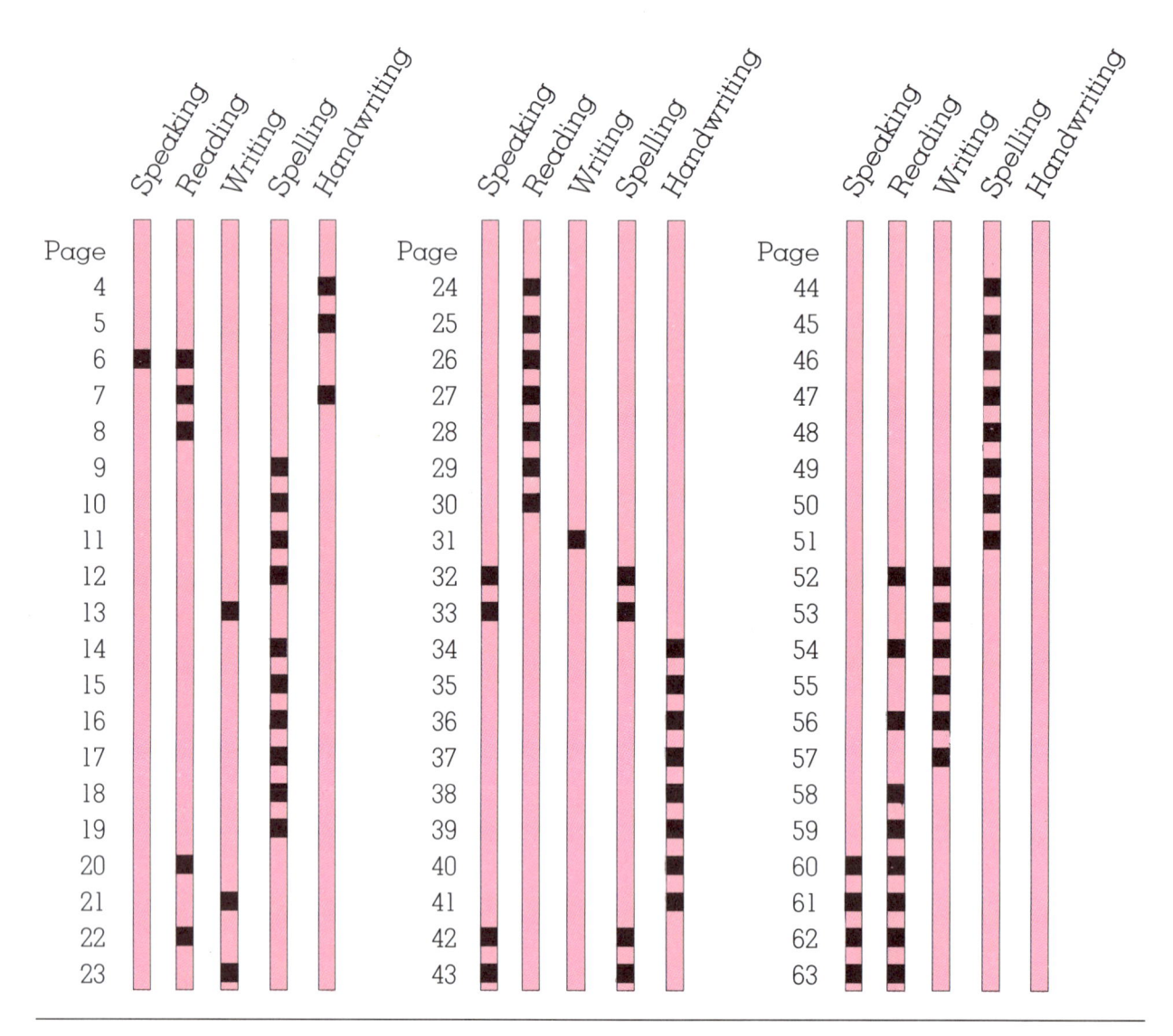

Page	Speaking	Reading	Writing	Spelling	Handwriting
4					■
5					■
6	■	■			
7		■			■
8		■			
9				■	
10				■	
11				■	
12				■	
13			■		
14				■	
15				■	
16				■	
17				■	
18				■	
19				■	
20		■			
21			■		
22		■			
23			■		

Page	Speaking	Reading	Writing	Spelling	Handwriting
24		■			
25		■			
26		■			
27		■			
28					
29					
30					
31			■		
32	■			■	
33	■				
34				■	
35				■	
36				■	
37				■	
38					
39					
40					
41					
42	■				
43		■		■	

Page	Speaking	Reading	Writing	Spelling	Handwriting
44				■	
45					
46					
47				■	
48				■	
49				■	
50					
51				■	
52	■	■	■		
53		■			
54		■	■		
55			■		
56			■		
57			■		
58		■			
59		■			
60	■	■			
61	■	■	■		
62		■	■		
63		■	■		

Oxford University Press, Walton Street, Oxford OX2 6DP
Oxford New York Toronto
Delhi Bombay Calcutta Madras Karachi
Kuala Lumpur Singapore Hong Kong Tokyo
Nairobi Dar es Salaam Cape Town
Melbourne Auckland Madrid
and associated companies in
Berlin Ibadan

Oxford is a trade mark of Oxford University Press
© Louis Fidge 1992
First published 1992
Reprinted 1992

ISBN 0 19 838102 6

Designed by Plum Design, Southampton
Illustrations by Lynda Knott and Jason Smith

Printed in Hong Kong

All rights reserved. No part of this publication may be reproduced, stored in a retrieval system, or transmitted, in any form or by any means, without the prior permission in writing of Oxford University Press. Within the U.K., exceptions are allowed in respect of any fair dealing for the purpose of research or private study, or criticism or review, as permitted under the Copyright, Designs and Patents Act, 1988, or in the case of reprographic reproduction in accordance with the terms of licenses issued by the Copyright Licensing Agency. Enquiries concerning reproduction outside those terms and in other countries should be sent to the Rights Department, Oxford University Press, at the address above.